A Question of Science

Why, Doesn't the Moon Fall out of the Sky?

And other
questions
about FORCES

Anna Claybourne

CRABTREE
PUBLISHING COMPANY
WWW.CRABTREEBOOKS.COM

CRABTREE
PUBLISHING COMPANY
WWW.CRABTREEBOOKS.COM

Published in Canada
Crabtree Publishing
616 Welland Ave.
St. Catharines, Ontario
L2M 5V6

Published in the United States
Crabtree Publishing
347 Fifth Avenue
Suite 1402–145
New York, NY 10016

Published in 2021 by Crabtree Publishing Company

First published in 2020 by Wayland
© Hodder and Stoughton 2020

Author: Anna Claybourne

Editorial Director: Kathy Middleton

Editor: Julia Bird

Proofreader: Petrice Custance

Design and illustration: Matt Lilly

Cover design: Matt Lilly

Production coordinator and
  Prepress technician: Tammy McGarr

Print coordinator: Katherine Berti

Printed in the U.S.A./082020/CG20200601

Picture credits
Aclosund Historic 5tr; E R Degginger 15br; Granger Historical Pictures Archive 26t; Malcolm Haines 16-17c; ITAR-TASS 28l; Science History Images 18bl; SPL 11b. Jelena Ivanovic 4cl; Christian Weiß 13t; Yinan Zhang 22cl. NASA: 5cb. David Shale 29t. ajlatan 25c; Andrey Armyagov & NASA 27b; Baronov E & NASA 1tr, 6t, 7c, 7cr,7br,27t; Denis Dryashkin 14t inside bowl b; Artem Egorov 14bl; Elenarts 9br; Germanskydiver 21c; Halfpoint 12bl; hsagencia 12br; irin-k 24br; Suphanat Khumsap 14t inside bowl t; Laborant 15tl, 15tr inside bowl; Dmitry Lobanov 24bl; Jan Miko 10t; Moomusician 21b; Nerthuz 9bc, 27c & NASA; Nicku 5cr, 17br, 29b; Nutchanon Shi 23; Wanchai Orsuk 12t; Pretty Vectors 22cr; Mauro Rodrigues 5br; Prachaya Roekdeethaweesab 5cl; robert_s & NASA 26b, 29cl; Edu Silva 2ev 28r; Spaxiax 4cr, 4br; Alex Staroseltsev 1b, 29cr; Maksim Toome 9c; YuRi Photolife 18-19c; Zonda 11t, 14t, 14br, 15tr.Wayland

Library and Achives Canada Cataloguing in Publication

Title: Why doesn't the moon fall out of the sky? : and other questions about forces / Anna Claybourne.
Names: Claybourne, Anna, author.
Description: Series statement: A question of science | Includes index.
Identifiers: Canadiana (print) 20200254812 | Canadiana (ebook) 20200254863 | ISBN 9780778779100 (softcover) | ISBN 9780778777106 (hardcover) | ISBN 9781427125422 (HTML)
Subjects: LCSH: Mechanics—Juvenile literature. | LCSH: Mechanics—Miscellanea—Juvenile literature. | LCSH: Force and energy—Juvenile literature. | LCSH: Force and energy—Miscellanea—Juvenile literature. | LCGFT: Trivia and miscellanea.
Classification: LCC QC127.4 .C53 2020 | DDC j531—dc23

Library of Congress Cataloging-in-Publication Data

Names: Claybourne, Anna, author.
Title: Why doesn't the moon fall out of the sky? : and other questions about forces / Anna Claybourne.
Description: New York : Crabtree Publishing Company, 2021. | Series: A question of science | First published in 2020 by Wayland.
Identifiers: LCCN 2020023418 (print) | LCCN 2020023419 (ebook) | ISBN 9780778777106 (hardcover) | ISBN 9780778779100 (paperback) | ISBN 9781427125422 (ebook)
Subjects: LCSH: Force and energy--Juvenile literature.
Classification: LCC QC73.4 .C51657 2021 (print) | LCC QC73.4 (ebook) | DDC 531/.6--dc23
LC record available at https://lccn.loc.gov/2020023418
LC ebook record available at https://lccn.loc.gov/2020023419

Contents

What is a force?

Forces are the pushes and pulls that make things move, stop moving, change direction, or stay still. Whatever's happening, forces are making it happen.

Even when you're sitting still like this, a lot of forces are at work:

● **Gravity** is pulling you down
● **Friction** makes you able to hold your book
● You're being squeezed by **air pressure** from the air all around you
● Even inside your brain, forces make signals zoom around between your brain cells, so you can understand what you're looking at.

To see a force in action, find something small and unbreakable, such as an eraser.

Pick it up...

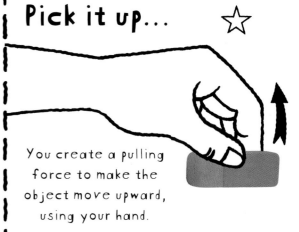

You create a pulling force to make the object move upward, using your hand.

Now drop it!

When you let go, another force pulls the object back down—the force of gravity.

Understanding forces

Scientists have been studying forces for centuries to find out how they work.

Agnes Pockels (1862-1935) did experiments on the **surface tension** of water.

I ALSO DISCOVERED JUPITER'S MOONS!

Isaac Newton (1642-1727), the most famous forces scientist of all time, came up with many rules and formulas that show how forces work.

Galileo Galilei (1564-1642) worked on how things fall and speed up.

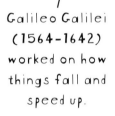

I HELPED PUT HUMANS ON THE MOON!

Katherine Johnson (1918-2020) calculated flight paths and **orbits** for spacecraft.

Inventions and discoveries

Understanding forces allows us to invent, build, and control all kinds of useful inventions, too...

Rockets

Bicycles   Brakes

Seesaws

Food processors

Helicopters

Bridges   Roller coasters

AND ROBOTS! THE LIST IS ENDLESS!

Why doesn't the Moon fall out of the sky?

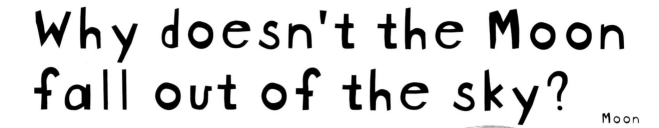

The Moon is a humongous ball made of about 16,200 trillion pounds (73,500 trillion kg). So have you ever wondered...

What's holding it up??

The Moon is Earth's constant companion, always sailing peacefully around the sky.

But HOW?

Earth has a powerful pulling force called gravity.

Gravity pulls you and other objects down toward the ground.

WOOF!
WOOF!
WOOF!

Moon

Mass

All objects have **mass**, which is the amount of **matter**, or stuff, that makes up the object. The more mass an object has, the more gravity it has.

Earth is a huge planet with a lot of mass. Its powerful gravity reaches far out into space.

The Moon is smaller than Earth, but it is pretty big. It has its own gravity, too.

LET ME GO!

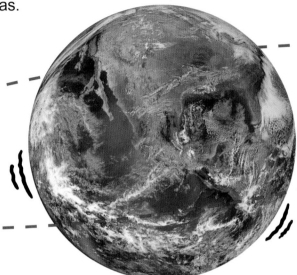

As the Moon moves, it tries to pull away in a straight line.

The gravities of both the Earth and Moon pull on each other. So, you might think they would just pull and pull until they crashed together...right?

However...

There's another force involved, too. The Moon is also moving at a high speed.

As the Moon zooms forward, it tries to pull away from Earth and fly off in a straight line. At the same time, gravity is also pulling the Moon toward Earth. This keeps the two forces in balance, so the Moon just keeps orbiting, or circling, Earth instead.

Orbits are everywhere!

Other planets also have moons orbiting them. The planets themselves orbit around the Sun. Humans send rockets and **satellites** into orbit, too. For example, the International Space Station (ISS) is spacecraft in orbit 248 miles (400 km) above Earth. Scientists live aboard it for months at a time.

ISS

Why does rubbing your hands together warm them up?

Brrrrr...

It's freezing and you've forgotten your gloves! Rub your hands together, and they should start to feel a bit warmer.

This handy heating method exists thanks to one of the most important forces of all: friction.

The rubbing force

Friction is a force that slows down or stops things when they rub, scrape, or slide together.

For example...

- Rubber gloves help you grip a tight jar lid
- Brakes rub against the wheels to slow down a bike
- Sneakers grip the ground.

Basically, if it wasn't for friction, we'd all be slipping and sliding around all over the place!

Rough stuff

Friction happens because surfaces are never completely smooth. Even if they look and feel smooth, through a microscope you'd see they have a rough surface.

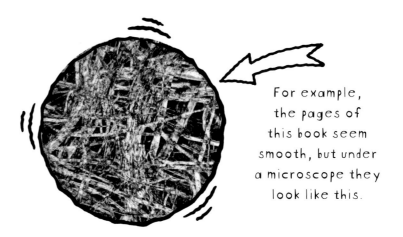

For example, the pages of this book seem smooth, but under a microscope they look like this.

But where does the heat come from?

When surfaces rub together, they get pushed and squeezed. This makes the **molecules** that make up the **materials** start moving around faster. When the molecules in a material move faster, the material becomes hotter—and that's what happens to your hands.

Burning up!

Friction can sometimes make things a LOT hotter than warm hands on a winter's day. For example,

... if you slide down a rope too fast, it makes your hands so hot you get a "friction burn" ...

...and rubbing sticks together can (eventually) start a fire!

Hot money!

This simple experiment will amaze you!

Put two matching coins on a pad of paper. Put one index finger on one coin, and one on the other.

Hold one coin still and rub the other one hard back and forth on the paper for ten seconds.

Compare the coins. Is one warmer?

Why don't pond skaters fall in?

Look closely at a pond on a summer day and you'll see insects called pond skaters zipping around on the surface.

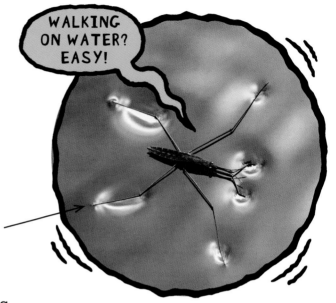

They're not floating like boats (see pages 14-15). They're actually STANDING on the water!

You can even see the water surface dipping where the pond skater's feet press on it. It's as if the water has a thin, stretchy skin.

Where's the skin?
Water doesn't actually have a skin. If it did, you'd find it in your glass when you had a drink.

Eeeww!

Instead, water just acts as if it has a skin, because of surface tension.

Look inside...

Water, like everything else, is made of tiny molecules. Something called cohesive forces pulls the molecules toward each other.

At the water's surface, the forces can only pull each molecule to the sides and below, not above.

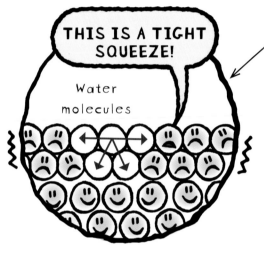

THIS IS A TIGHT SQUEEZE!

Water molecules

In the middle of the water, the forces pull each molecule in all directions.

With fewer directions to be pulled at the surface, the molecules pull closer together and form a skin called surface tension. It will support the weight of an insect, but surface tension is quite weak. You can still break through it easily.

Try it yourself...

To test surface tension, fill a bowl with water, wait until it's still, then gently lower a small paper clip onto the surface.

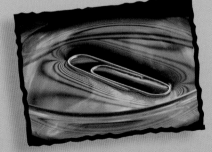

Metal objects such as paper clips don't float, but the surface tension can hold them up.

Drip... drop...

Surface tension is also the reason water forms round drops. A small amount of water pulls itself into a ball. If it's on a flat surface, it forms a dome.

How does a parachute save your life?

Jumping out of a plane without a parachute would be seriously bad news. But if you had a parachute, you'd be fine—even if you fell thousands of feet!

Tiny air **particles**

Going down!

If you jump out of a plane, Earth's gravity pulls you down, so you fall quickly toward the ground.

But, as you fall through the air, you hit millions of tiny, invisible air particles. They push against you and slow you down a bit (but not much).

This is called **air resistance** or **drag**. It's a type of friction (see pages 8–9).

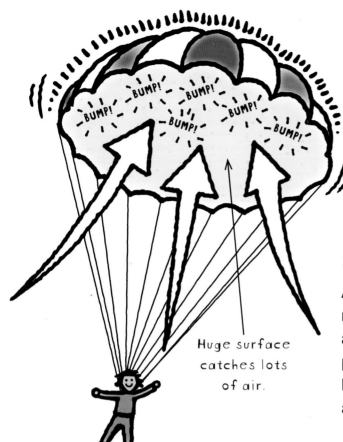

Huge surface catches lots of air.

Slow me down!

The bigger your surface area, the more particles you'll hit, and the slower you'll go. A parachute has a really big surface area, and lots of air resistance, making the fall slow enough to be safe.

Speed me up!

Air resistance slows down anything that moves through air, such as planes, cars, and bikes. Vehicles are designed with pointed, smooth, **streamlined** shapes because it reduces air resistance and allows them to move faster..

Streamlined shapes let air flow past them easily.

Water resistance

The same thing happens in water. The resistance is even stronger since water is thicker than air. Many sea animals, such as penguins, have a streamlined shape to help them swim faster.

Streamlined penguin

We make submarines this shape, too.

How can a metal boat float?

Container ship

Steel nail

Drop a steel nail into water and it will sink. Yet a massive, steel container ship floats on the ocean. What's that about?

To see why this happens, you have to start with why things float. It all has to do with how **dense** materials are. Density is how heavy an object is for its size.

Why steel sinks

To float, an object has to be less dense than water.

Thirty-four ounces
(1 liter)
of water like
this weighs
2.2 pounds (1 kg).

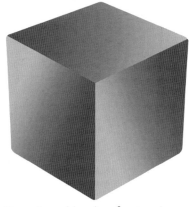

Here's a block of steel
the exact same size,
but it weighs 17.4 pounds
(7.9 kg)! Its material
is much denser...

...so it would sink
in the water!

Why wood floats

Now let's try it with a block of wood the same size.

The wood block weighs about 0.88 pounds (0.4 kg). It's less dense than water...

...so it floats!

Upthrust

When you put an object in water, the water pushes back up against it with a force called **upthrust**. The upthrust can only hold up objects that are less dense than water. It can't support denser objects, so they sink back down.

Brilliant boats

HOWEVER, boats can float, even steel boats, because of their shape.

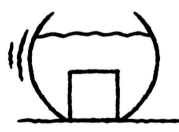 

A solid lump of steel sinks, because it's denser than water.

But a boat is shaped like a bowl, with air in the middle.

The density of the whole shape isn't just steel. It also includes the air inside. All the air makes the overall density much lower—

so the boat floats!

Floating metals

The metals lithium, sodium, and potassium are actually less dense than water and can float. However, they don't make great boats because they explode when they touch water!

BANG!

How can a plane fly upside down?

You might have heard that planes can fly because of the shape of their wings. But if that's how planes fly, then flying upside down should make them fall to the ground, right?

But many planes CAN fly upside down... like this one!

How?

Many aircraft wings do have a special shape, called an **airfoil**. It's shaped like this:

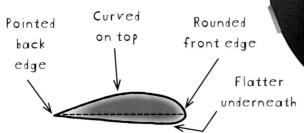

Pointed back edge

Curved on top

Rounded front edge

Flatter underneath

This shape makes air zoom over the top of the wing much faster than the bottom. Faster-moving air presses less hard, so there's less air pressure on the top of the wing than on the bottom. This gives the wing **lift**.

Lift is a force that pushes upward, against gravity.

But...

There's something else that's actually much more important for making a plane fly, and that's the angle of the wings.

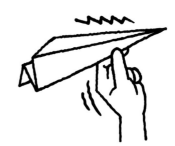

After all, a paper airplane just has flat wings. But it will fly for a while if you throw it at the right angle.

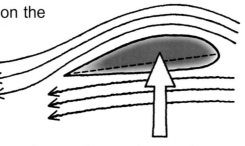

Angle of attack

As a plane flies along, its wings are angled slightly upward at the front.

(1) The air flowing below the wings is pushed downward.

(2) The air flowing over the wing is forced downward too, as it flows off the back of the sloping wing.

Wings angled upward

MIND MY HEAD!

When a force pushes on an object, the object pushes back with the same force. So, as the wings push air down, the air pushes back against them and the wing is lifted.

Invert!

Stunt pilots call upside-down flight "inverted." To do it, they have to fly with the nose of the plane pointing up slightly, so that the wings are still angled upward.

Equal and opposite

It was the brilliant scientist Isaac Newton who explained how, when a force acts on something, it pushes back with an equal force in the opposite direction.

IT'S CALLED MY (NEWTON'S) THIRD LAW OF MOTION!

Why can't people grow as big as dinosaurs?

Brachiosaurus

Imagine being 39 feet (12 m) tall—as tall as a four-story building! Giants in myths and movies can be this big and so were some dinosaurs.

So why aren't there any giant humans?

Real-life giants

The tallest man on record was Robert Wadlow, who grew to be 8.9 feet (2.72 m) tall!

Average human height is around 5 feet 5 inches (1.651 m). Wadlow did look giant, but he was still less than twice the average height for a human. Real giants, the height of a brachiosaurus, don't exist for a very good reason...
...FORCES!

Life in 3-D

If you were 39 feet (12 m) tall like a brachiosaurus, you'd be about seven times taller than average. But humans are **3-D** objects. If you were seven times taller, you wouldn't just be seven times heavier. You'd be much, MUCH heavier.

Here's how it works.

1 Think of a cube…

2 Now imagine a cube twice as tall. It wouldn't just be twice as heavy–it would be **8** times heavier.

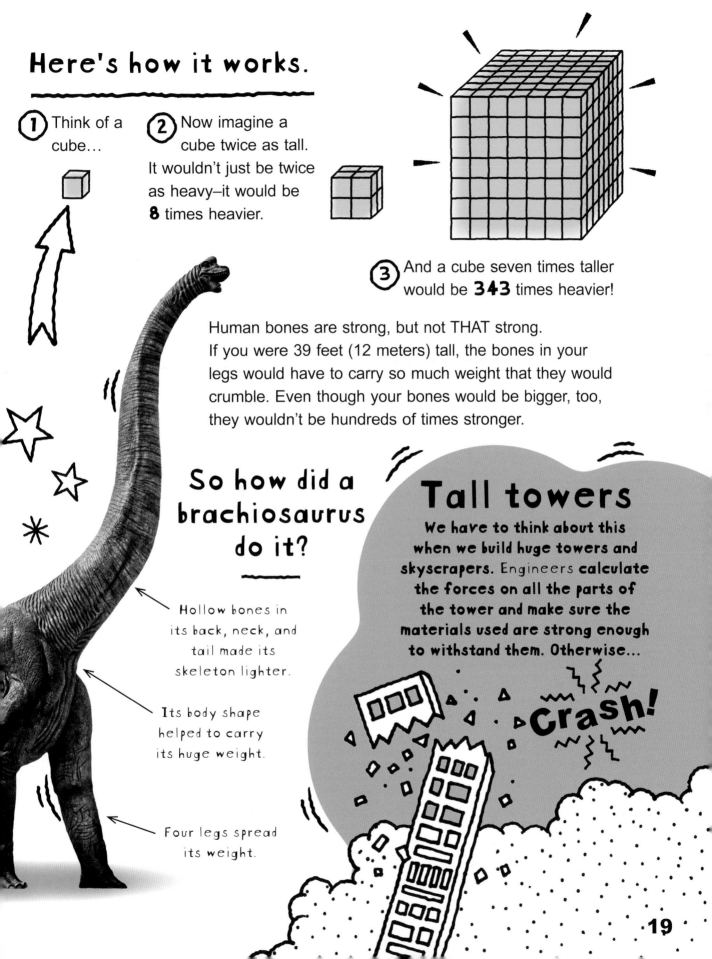

3 And a cube seven times taller would be **343** times heavier!

Human bones are strong, but not THAT strong. If you were 39 feet (12 meters) tall, the bones in your legs would have to carry so much weight that they would crumble. Even though your bones would be bigger, too, they wouldn't be hundreds of times stronger.

So how did a brachiosaurus do it?

Hollow bones in its back, neck, and tail made its skeleton lighter.

Its body shape helped to carry its huge weight.

Four legs spread its weight.

Tall towers

We have to think about this when we build huge towers and skyscrapers. Engineers **calculate the forces** on all the parts of the tower and make sure the materials used are strong enough to withstand them. Otherwise…

Crash!

Why is falling off a cliff so deadly?

Jumping off a chair or a small wall is (usually!) pretty safe, but falling off a cliff or high building definitely isn't. The reason is all to do with gravity.

Falling down... speeding up

When an object falls, Earth's gravity pulls it down to the ground. But as objects fall, they also accelerate, or move faster and faster. This is called the **acceleration** of gravity, or **g**.

Here's how **g** works. Imagine dropping a small rock off a cliff.

(Just imagine it, though. DON'T ever do it, as it could land on someone!)

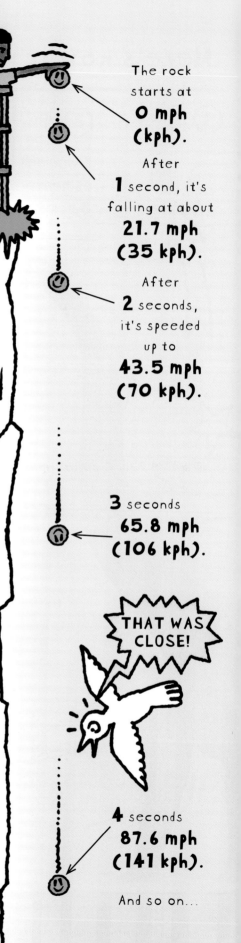

The rock starts at **0 mph (kph)**.

After **1** second, it's falling at about **21.7 mph (35 kph)**.

After **2** seconds, it's speeded up to **43.5 mph (70 kph)**.

3 seconds **65.8 mph (106 kph)**.

THAT WAS CLOSE!

4 seconds **87.6 mph (141 kph)**.

And so on...

If a rock fell off a 328-foot (100 m) high cliff, it would take about 4.5 seconds to get to the bottom. By the time it landed, it would be traveling at 98 mph (158 kph). That's FAST—as fast as a high-speed train.

THAT WAS QUICK!

Top speed!

In real life, falling objects don't keep speeding up forever. As an object falls faster, it hits the air harder, and there's more air resistance. Eventually, the object reaches its maximum possible speed, which is called its terminal velocity.

For a falling human, such as a skydiver, terminal velocity is about 124.2 mph (200 kph).

Sky spider

DON'T WORRY, I'LL BE FINE!

Smaller, lighter animals have more surface area for their weight, so there's more air resistance. They don't reach a very high speed.

So, for example, a spider could fall off a skyscraper and survive without injury.

How can a magnet pull something it's not... touching?

Magnets pull toward each other, or push each other away, depending on which way round you hold them.

It's like magic! Or IS it.....?

Fridge magnet

Maglev train

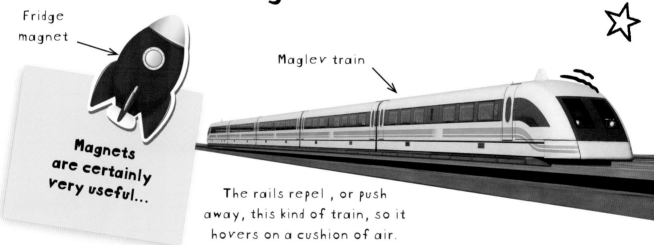

Magnets are certainly very useful...

The rails repel , or push away, this kind of train, so it hovers on a cushion of air.

So what's happening?

Magnetism isn't magical. It's just another type of force.

Here's how it works...

Materials are all made up of tiny **atoms**, which have even tinier particles called electrons whizzing around them. In some atoms, the electrons create a pulling force. But usually atoms are all jumbled up and pointing in different directions, so any pulling forces cancel each other out.

Electrons

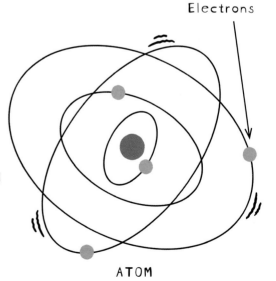

ATOM

In a magnetic material, the pulling forces can line up, creating a single bigger pulling force in one direction.

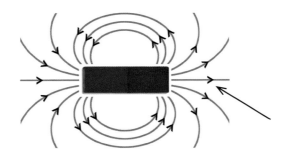

The area of force around the magnet is called the magnetic field.

Push or pull?

Magnets have two ends, called the north and south poles.

North pole

South pole

The north pole of one magnet and the south pole of another magnet will attract, or pull each other.

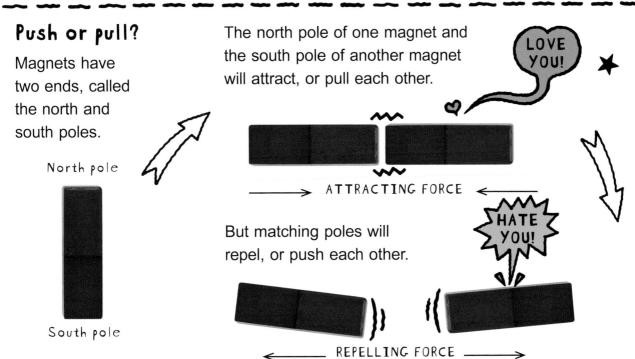

LOVE YOU!

ATTRACTING FORCE

But matching poles will repel, or push each other.

HATE YOU!

REPELLING FORCE

Faraway forces

Magnets can push and pull across a gap, because the pulling forces in the atoms can do this. How this actually works is still not totally understood, even by scientists. But it's not that strange.

If you think about it, magnetism is like gravity (see pages 20-21). It can pull without touching you.

Magnetic metals

Magnets also attract some metals, such as the steel in a paper clip. When a magnet pulls on these metals, the objects can become magnetic too.

This means you can use one magnet to magnetize a chain of paper clips.

23

How does the tablecloth trick work?

Can you really pull a tablecloth out from under a set of plates and cups, leaving them all where they were?

The answer is yes, but you have to do it right. DON'T try this at home! Try the easier experiment on the opposite page instead.

How it's done

To make the trick work, the secret is to pull the tablecloth as hard and suddenly as possible. If you pull it too slowly, everything will get pulled off and...

Smash!

But why?

Inertia

Inertia is one of the laws of motion explained by Isaac Newton (see page 17). It basically means that objects will try to keep doing whatever they're doing. For example, if an object is moving, it will keep going, like this ball...

...unless other forces slow it down, stop it, or change its direction.

Splosh!

Stay still!

If an object is still, it will stay still…

…unless forces act on it to move it...

...LIKE THIS!

TA-DAAA!

Staying on the table

In the tablecloth trick, the objects on the table won't move unless there's a force strong enough to overcome their inertia.

Friction makes the objects grip the tablecloth. If you pull it slowly, this friction makes the objects move with it.

But there isn't enough friction to make the objects move really fast. So if you whip the tablecloth out in a split second, they'll stay still!

(It works best if the tablecloth has a smooth, flat edge.)

Pull the paper

Instead of a tablecloth, try this slightly less risky version.

Cut a piece of paper about the size of a playing card. Put it on top of a clean, dry bottle, and stack several coins on top.

Now try to pull the paper out fast, leaving the coins on the bottle.

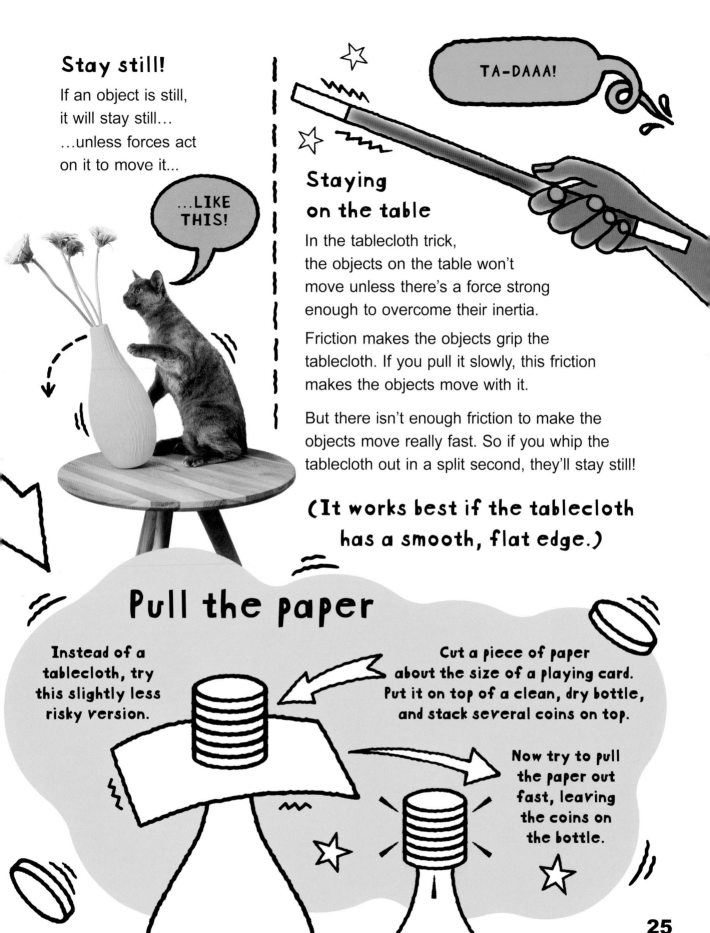

25

Why can you jump higher on the Moon?

 Boing!

 Boing!

Boing!

"...walking on the Moon is like walking on a giant trampoline..."

– according to astronaut Harrison Schmitt, who went there in 1972.

You can jump higher on the Moon, and you fall back down more slowly. That's not because the Moon is bouncy.

It's because you actually weigh less on the Moon!

What is weight?

You might think your weight is the same wherever you are, but weight doesn't work like that.

Your mass stays the same wherever you are. Mass is the amount of matter, or stuff, in an object. For example, your mass might be 79 lbs (36 kg).

But weight actually means how much gravity pulls on an object.

Mass:
79 lbs
(36 kg)
Weight:
79 lbs
(36 kg)

On Earth, you'd weigh 79 lbs (36 kg)...

but on the Moon you'd weigh much less, because the Moon is smaller and has weaker gravity.

In fact, on the Moon, you'd only weigh about one sixth of what you do on Earth.

YIP-PEE!

Stuck on Jupiter

If you traveled to a much bigger planet, such as Jupiter, where gravity is much stronger, it wouldn't be like a trampoline at all. It would be more like being stuck to the ground.

I FEEL SO HEAVY I CAN'T MOVE!

(Actually, it wouldn't be quite like this, because Jupiter is mostly gas and liquid. There wouldn't be any solid ground to be stuck to. But if there was, it would be hard to stand up!)

Floating free

As you move farther away from a planet (or Moon), the pull of its gravity on you gets weaker. In outer space, you're so far from any planet that there's hardly any gravity at all. This weak gravity is called **microgravity**. This is why astronauts in space feel weightless, and can float around in all directions.

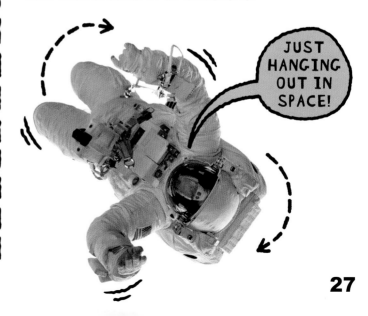

JUST HANGING OUT IN SPACE!

Quick-fire questions

How do rockets take off?

Rockets work using Newton's famous law of equal and opposite reactions. When a rocket launches, it burns a huge amount of fuel, shooting gases downward out of its engine at high speed. As the rocket pushes out the gases, the gases push back against the rocket, forcing it upward.

Is Earth a giant magnet?

Yes, Earth has a powerful magnetic field. Liquid iron at the center of Earth has **electric currents** flowing in it. As Earth spins, this electricity creates a strong magnetic force.

How do tightrope walkers stay up?

An object can balance if its center of gravity, or the middle point of its mass, is directly above the base it stands on. On a tightrope, your base is very narrow. You have to keep shifting your weight to keep your central point directly above the tightrope.

Whooosh!

Why can't we feel air pressure?

The weight of air in Earth's **atmosphere** creates a lot of air pressure. We don't notice it because we're used to it, and our bodies have **evolved** to have a similar pressure inside. However, if you go deep underwater, you feel very squashed because water pressure is even stronger. But a deep-sea creature such as a giant squid or anglerfish feels fine, because it has evolved to cope with that pressure.

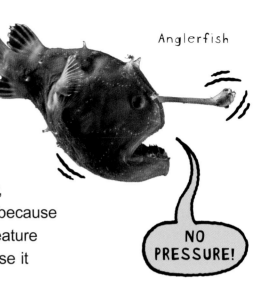

Anglerfish

NO PRESSURE!

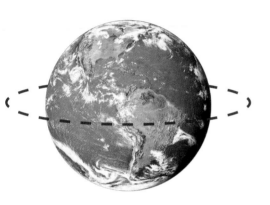

Did Isaac Newton really discover gravity when an apple fell on his head?

MMM... APPLE PIE!

This is a famous story, but it isn't quite accurate. Everyone knows things fall to the ground, so Newton didn't really "discover" gravity. However, he did describe how seeing apples falling from trees made him come up with ideas about gravity. He did not say that an apple fell on his head (although it's possible, of course!).

Why can't we feel Earth spinning?

Earth rotates once every 24 hours, which means that you're zooming around on it at about 621 mph (1,000 kph) on average. (It varies, depending on how close to the **equator** you are.) However, Earth's atmosphere is spinning with it, so you don't feel as if you're going fast.

Glossary

3-D Short for three-dimensional, describes an object that has length, width, and height

acceleration The rate at which an object speeds up as it moves or falls

airfoil The shape of an aircraft wing that helps to provide lift

air pressure The force of the air all around us pressing on people and objects

air resistance A force that slows down a moving object as air pushes against it

atmosphere The layer of gases all around Earth

atoms Tiny units that matter is made up of

dense How heavy something is for its size

drag Another name for air resistance

electric current The flow of an electric charge from one point to another

engineer Someone who designs or maintains buildings or other structures

equator An invisible line that runs around the center of Earth

evolved Developed and changed over time

friction A force that slows down or stops objects as they scrape or rub together

gravity A force that pulls all objects toward each other

inertia The way an object will tend to stay doing what it's doing, whether it's still or moving

lift A force that pushes an object, such as an aircraft wing, upward

magnetism A force that makes some objects pull together or push apart

mass The amount of matter that an object contains

materials The stuff that everything is made from

matter The stuff that everything is made up of

microgravity Very weak gravity, in which you feel weightless

molecules Units of matter made from atoms joined together

orbits The paths taken by objects as they circle other objects

particles Units that make up atoms

satellites Objects that orbit around other objects, especially a human-made satellite such as a space station

streamlined Having a long, pointed shape that helps an object move through air or water more easily

surface tension A force that makes molecules at the surface of water pull together, making the water behave as if it has a thin skin

upthrust A force that pushes upward on an object in a liquid or gas.

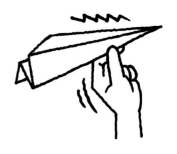

Learning More

Books

Chatterton, Crystal. *Awesome Science Experiments for Kids*. Rockridge Press, 2018.

Claybourne, Anna. *Gut-Wrenching Gravity and Other Fatal Forces*. Crabtree Publishing, 2013.

Claybourne, Anna. *Recreate Discoveries about Forces*. Crabtree Publishing, 2018.

Rowell, Rebecca. *Forces and Motion Through Infographics*. Lerner Publications, 2018.

Websites

www.dkfindout.com/us/science/ forces-and-motion/what-is-force/
Lots of clear, simple forces facts, plus pictures and a quiz.

www.fizzicseducation.com.au/ category/150-science-experiments/ force-movement-experiments/
Fun forces and movement experiments to try.

www.sciencebuddies.org/stem-activities
Amazing ideas for STEM projects and experiments.

www.stevespanglerscience.com/lab/ categories/experiments/forces-and-motion/
Forces and motion activities from Steve Spangler Science.

Index